MW00487912

# Financial Crisis Inquiry Commission Staff Audiotape of Interview with Warren Buffett Berkshire Hathaway

*May 26, 2010*

**INTERVIEWER:** Thank you. Mr. Buffett, we're with the staff of the Financial Crisis Inquiry Commission. We were formed by Congress in 2009 to investigate the causes of the financial crisis both globally and domestically and to do a report, due at the end of this year – December 15, 2010 – to the President and to Congress, which we also plan to release to the American public. We're tasked not only with investigating the causes of the financial crisis but looking at specific issues that Congress has enumerated in the Fraud Enforcement Recovery Act which formed the commission. The commission is a bipartisan commission, six Democrats and four Republican commissioners, and we are with the staff of the commission. We wanted to ask you a few questions today and get your views and your insights so that we may better understand the causes of the financial crisis. In addition, we would like to ask you a few questions about Moody's as well, since you are a significant shareholder in Moody's. And if you don't mind, let's ask first about Moody's specifically.

**INTERVIEWER:** I understand, sir, that in 1999 and in February of 2000, you invested in Dun and Bradstreet.

**WARREN BUFFETT:** That's correct. I don't have the dates, but that sounds right.

**INTERVIEWER:** Yes, sir. And am I correct, sir, in saying that you made no purchases after Moody's spun off from Dun and Bradstreet?

**WARREN BUFFETT:** I believe that's correct.

**INTERVIEWER:** What kind of due diligence did you and your staff do when you first purchased Dun and Bradstreet in 1999 and then again in 2000?

**WARREN BUFFETT:** There is no staff. I make all the investment decisions and I do all my own analysis. And basically it was an evaluation both of Dun and Bradstreet and Moody's, but of the economics of their business. And I never met with anybody. Dun and Bradstreet had a very good business and Moody's had an even better business. And basically the single most important decision in evaluating a business is pricing power. You've got the power to raise prices without losing business to a competitor, and you've got a very good business. And if you have to have a prayer session before raising the price by a tenth of a cent (laughs), then you got a terrible business. And I've been in both and I know the difference.

**INTERVIEWER:** Now, you've described the importance of quality management in your investing decisions, and I know your mentor, Benjamin Graham – I happen to have read his book – as well has described the importance of management. What attracted you to the management of Moody's when you made your initial investments?

**WARREN BUFFETT:** I knew nothing about the management of Moody's. I've also said many times in annual reports and elsewhere that one of the many, but with reputation of for brilliance in him gets hooked up with a business with a reputation of bad economics, it's the reputation of the business that remains intact. If you've got a good enough business, if you have a monopoly newspaper, if you have a network television station, I'm talking in the past, you know, your idiot nephew could run it. And if you've got a really good business, it doesn't make any difference. It makes some difference maybe in capital allocation or something of the sort, but the extraordinary business does not require good management.

I'm not making any reference to Moody's management. I didn't know them, but it really, you know, if you own the only newspaper in town up till the last five years or so, you have pricing power and you didn't have to go to the office.

**INTERVIEWER:** And do you have any opinion, sir, of how well management of Moody's has performed?

**WARREN BUFFETT:** It's hard to evaluate when you have a business that has that much pricing power. I mean, they have done very well in terms of huge returns on tangible assets, almost infinite. And they have, they have grown along with a business that generally capital markets became more active and all that. So in the end--and they've raised prices--we're a customer of Moody's too, so I see this from both sides--and an unwilling customer--but we're a customer nevertheless. And what I see as a customer is reflected in what's happened in their financial record.

**INTERVIEWER:** And I've seen in many places where you've been referred to as a passive investor of Moody's. Is that a fair characterization, and what sort of interactions and communications have you had with the Board and with management of Moody's?

**WARREN BUFFETT:** At the very start there was a fellow named Cliff Alexander who was the Chairman of Dun and Bradstreet while they were breaking it up. He met me--I met him in connection with something else years earlier. So we had a lunch at one time, but he wasn't really an operating manager; he was there sort to oversee the breakup of the situation. Since we really owned stock in both Dun and Bradstreet and Moody's when they got split up, I'd never been in Moody's offices. I don't think I've ever initiated a call to them. I would say that three or four times as part of a general roadshow their CEO and the investor relations person would stop by and they think they have to do that. I have no interest in it basically and I never requested a meeting. It just, it was part of what they thought investor relations were all about. And we don't believe much in that.

**INTERVIEWER:** What about any Board members? Have you pressed for the election of any Board members to Moody's Board?

**WARREN BUFFETT:** No, I have no interest in it.

**INTERVIEWER:** And we've talked about just verbal communications. Have you sent any letters or submitted any memos or ideas for strategy decisions to Moody's?

**WARREN BUFFETT:** No, no. If I thought they needed me, I wouldn't have bought the stock (laughs).

**INTERVIEWER:** In 2006 Moody's began to re-purchase its shares, buying back its shares that were outstanding, and they did so from 2006 to 2008 according to our records. Why didn't you sell back your shares to Moody's at that time? I know subsequently in 2009 you've sold some shares, but from '06 to '09 during the buy-back, did you consider selling your shares back, and if so, why didn't you?

**WARREN BUFFETT:** Oh, I thought they had an extraordinary business, and you know, they still have an extraordinary business now subject to a different threat which we'll get into later, I'm sure. But I made a mistake in that it got to very lofty heights and we didn't sell. It wouldn't have made any difference whether we were selling to them or selling in the market. But there are very few businesses that had the competitive position that Moody's and Standard and Poor's had; they both had the same position essentially. Very few businesses like that in the world. It's a natural duopoly to some extent; now that may get changed, but it has historically been a natural duopoly where anybody coming in and offering to cut their price in half had no chance of success. And there are not many businesses where somebody could come in to cut the price in half and somebody doesn't think about shifting. But that's the nature of the ratings business and it's a naturally obtained one. I mean, it's assisted by the fact that the two of them became the standard for regulators and all of that. So it's been assisted by the governmental actions over time. But it's a natural duopoly.

**INTERVIEWER:** Now, Mr. Buffett, you've been reported as saying that you don't use ratings.

**WARREN BUFFETT:** That's right.

**INTERVIEWER:** But the world does.

**WARREN BUFFETT:** That's right. But we pay for ratings which I don't like (laughs).

**INTERVIEWER:** My question is one more of policy and philosophy, and that is, would the

American economy be better off in the long run if credit ratings were not so embedded in our regulations and if market participants relied less on credit ratings?

**WARREN BUFFETT:** Well, I think it might be better off if everybody that invested significant sums of money did their own analysis, but that is not the way the world works. And regulators have a terrible problem in setting capital requirements, all of that sort of thing, without some kind of standards that they look to even if those are far from perfect standards. I can't really judge it perfectly from the regulators' standpoint. From the investors' standpoint, I think that investors should do their own analysis and we always do.

**INTERVIEWER:** Would you support the removal of references to credit ratings from regulations?

**WARREN BUFFETT:** That's a tough question. I mean, you get into--you get into, you know, how you regulate insurance companies and banks. And we are very significantly in the insurance business and we are told that we can only own triple B and above and different--there are all kinds of different rules in different states and even different countries. And those may serve as a crude tool to determine proper capital or to prevent buccaneers of one sort from going out and speculating, in the case of banks, with money that's obtained through a government guarantee. So that is not an easy question.

**INTERVIEWER:** As I mentioned at the outset, we're investigating the causes of the financial crisis and I would like to get your opinion as to whether credit ratings and their apparent failure to predict accurately credit quality of structured finance products like residential mortgage-backed securities and collateralized debt obligations. Did that failure or apparent failure cause or contribute to the financial crisis?

**WARREN BUFFETT:** It didn't cause it but there were a vast number of things that contributed to it. The basic cause was, you know, embedded in, partly in psychology, partly in reality, in a growing and finally pervasive belief that house prices couldn't go down. And everybody succumbed--virtually everybody succumbed to that. But that's--the only way you get a bubble is when basically a very high percentage of the population buys into some originally sound premise – and it's quite interesting how that develops – originally sound premise that becomes distorted as time passes, and people forget the original sound premise and start focusing solely on the price action. So the media, investors, mortgage bankers, the American public, me, you know, my neighbor, rating agencies, Congress, you name it. People overwhelmingly came to believe that house prices could not fall significantly. And since it was the biggest asset class in the country and it was the easiest class to borrow against, it created, you know, probably the biggest bubble in our history. It'll be a bubble that will be remembered along with South Sea bubble and [unintelligible] bubble.

**INTERVIEWER:** I do want to ask you some questions about the formation of that bubble, if I may ask a couple more on the rating agency side and then shift to that. And that is, do I take it, though, that you believe that at least the failure of the ratings contributed in some part to the financial crisis?

**WARREN BUFFETT:** But I do think it was--I think every aspect of society contributed to it virtually, but they fell prey to the same delusion that existed throughout the country eventually. And it meant that the models they had were no good. They didn't contemplate, but neither did the models in the minds of 300 million Americans contemplate what was going to happen.

**INTERVIEWER:** And similarly, sir, the ratings agencies, both Moody's and S&P, downgraded securities en masse in July of 2007, July, roughly starting around July 10, 2007, and then again in mid October of 2007. Many have pointed to these downgrades as contributing to the crisis. Do you believe that these downgrades, the sudden downgrades contributed to uncertainty in the market or the looming crisis?

**WARREN BUFFETT:** Well, I think that the realization by people that a bubble was starting to pop, and you know, everybody doesn't wake up a 6 a.m. on some morning and find it out. But Freddie Mac, Fannie Mae, they all felt different in the middle of 2007 than they did in the middle of 2006 or 2005. So people were watching a movie and they thought the movie had a happy ending, and all of a sudden the events on the screen started telling them something different. And different people in the audience picked it up at maybe different hours, different days, different weeks. But at some point the bubble popped.

And for different people it was, they were seeing it at slightly different times. But you can say the media's caused it too, if they say the bubble's popping, you know. The recognition of it by the rating agencies, I would say, you know, may have pulled a whole bunch of people that previously hadn't been paying much attention that it was happening. The report's coming out of Freddie and Fannie may have told people what was happening countrywide, and I think that was the summer of 2007 certainly was telling people that. So it was dawning on people in a way sort of that what they believed wasn't true.

**INTERVIEWER:** Now I read in one of your shareholder letters--I thought you appropriately said, "A pin lies in wait for every bubble."

**WARREN BUFFETT:** And this was the biggest one.

**INTERVIEWER:** When did you realize that there was a mortgage meltdown coming, and if so, what steps did you take to prepare for it? And if not, why were you unable, as one of the purportedly wisest investors in the United States, why were you unable to spot this massive bubble growing?

**WARREN BUFFETT:** The answer is, to the first part, was not soon enough (laughs). And it was something we talked about at our annual meetings, and I think one point I referred to it as a bubblette, I don't remember what year that was. But--and I talked about my home in Laguna where the implicit value of the land had gotten up to $30 million an acre or something like that, on that order. But the nature of bubbles is that, you know, with the Internet bubble I was aware of it too, but I didn't go and shorten stocks. I never shorted Internet stocks and I didn't short housing stocks. Looking back, you know, a) we don't short around here, but you know, if I'd seen what was coming, I might have behaved differently (laughs), including selling Moody's. Something's wrong.

**INTERVIEWER:** And we've obviously had bubbles in the past, as you pointed out, with the Internet bubble and others. But at least in recent times we've never had a financial crisis as severe as the one we're living through now. When did it dawn on you that this bubble was bursting and this financial crisis was going to be different than any others in recent times?

**WARREN BUFFETT:** Well, unfortunately, it's a gradual process, and you know, you get wise too late. When it really became apparent that, you know, that this was something like we'd never seen was in September 2008; that's when I said on CNBC, this is an economic Pearl Harbor. Well, it was an economic Pearl Harbor by definition. I meant that I hadn't seen it three months earlier because I didn't see a Pearl Harbor three months earlier. There were all kinds of developments, but the degree to which it would stop the financial system, you know, and then with the consequent overflow into the economy, you know, until September 2008, I didn't fully realize.

**INTERVIEWER:** What do you think it was, if you were to point to one of the single driving causes behind this bubble? What would you say?

**WARREN BUFFETT:** There's a really interesting aspect of this which will take a minute or two to explain, but my former boss, Ben Graham, in an observation 50 or so years ago to me that really stuck in my mind and now I've seen elements of it. He said you can get in a whole lot more trouble in investing with a sound premise than with a false premise. If you have some premise that the moon is made of green cheese or something, you know, it's ridiculous on its face. If you come up with a premise that common stocks have done better than bonds – and I wrote about this in a Fortune article in 2001. Because it was, there was a famous little book in 2001 by Edgar Lawrence Smith, in 1924, I think, by Edgar Lawrence Smith that made a study of common stocks versus bonds. And it showed, he started out with the idea that bonds would over-perform during deflation and common stocks would over-perform during inflation. He went back and studied a whole bunch of periods, and lo and behold, his original hypothesis was wrong. He found that common stocks always over-performed. And he started to think about it and why was that. Well, it was because there was a retained earnings factor. The dividend you got on stocks was the same as the yield on bonds, and on top of that you had retained earnings. So they over-performed. That became the underlying bulwark for the '29 bubble. People thought stocks were starting to be wonderful and they forgot the limitations of the original premise, which was that if stocks were yielding the same as bonds, that they had this going for them. So after a while the original premise – which becomes sort of the impetus for what later turns out to be a bubble – is forgotten and the price action takes over.

Now we saw the same thing in housing. It's a totally sound premise that houses will become worth more over time because the dollar becomes worth less. It isn't because, you know, construction costs go up, and it isn't because houses are so wonderful. It's because the dollar becomes worth less, that a house that was bought 40 years ago is worth more today than it was then. And since 66% or 67% of the people want to own their home and because you can borrow money on it and you're dreaming of buying a home, if you really believe that houses are going to go up in value, you buy one as soon as you can. And that's a very sound premise. It's related, of course, though, to houses selling at something like replacement price and not [unintelligible] of stripping inflation. So the sound premise it's a good idea to buy a house this year because it will probably cost more next year and you're going to want a home and the fact that you can finance it gets distorted over time if housing prices are going up 10% a year and inflation is a couple of percent a year. Soon the price action, or at some point the price action takes over, and you want to buy three houses and five houses, and you want to buy with nothing down, and you want to agree to payments that you can't make and all of that sort of thing because it doesn't make any difference; it's going to be worth more next year. And the lender feels the same way. Doesn't really make difference if it's a liar's loan or you don't have the income or something because even if they have to take it over, it'll be worth more next year. Once that gathers momentum and it gets reinforced by price action and the original premise is forgotten which it was in 1929.

The Internet, it's the same thing. The Internet was going to change our lives, but it didn't mean that every company was worth $50 billion that could dream up a prospectus and the price action becomes so important to people that it takes over their minds. And because housing was the largest single asset – around 22 trillion or something like on about, you know, a household wealth of 50 or 60 trillion or something like that in the United States – such a huge asset, so understandable to the public. They might not understand stocks or the Internet, you know, they might not understand tulip bulbs, but they understood houses and they wanted to buy one anyway. And the financing – and you could leverage up to the sky – it created a bubble like we've never seen. I wish I'd figured that out in 2005.

**INTERVIEWER:** This bubble, though, has been described as different from prior housing bubbles. And certainly the forces that you've described about prices and certainly the types of loans that you've described have been around for a while. What do you think, though, made this particular housing bubble different and what would you point to for the growth of this particular housing bubble? Some have pointed to cheap money, in essence; some have pointed to lack of regulation in the origination business; some have pointed to the drive from Wall Street for securitized mortgages and RMBS and then as collateral for CEOs. Others have pointed to government policy that created the housing bubble. What do you think created and caused this housing bubble?

**WARREN BUFFETT:** It's a great question to which I don't have a great answer. Why did the--I don't know whether the tulip bulb bubble was in 1610 or 20 but tulips had been around before and they'd always looked beautiful and people had wanted them on their tables and all that. And for some reason it gets to a critical mass, this critical point where price action alone starts dominating people's minds. And when your neighbor has made a lot of money by buying Internet stocks, you know, and your wife says that you're smarter than he is and he's richer than you are, you know, so why aren't you doing it. When that gets to a point, when day trading gets going –all of that sort of thing – very hard to point to what does it. I mean, it, you know, we've had hula hoops in this country, we've had pet rocks, I mean, you know, and this is the financial manifestation of, you know, a craze of sorts. And I--it's very hard to tell what got the--all the--you can name a lot of factors that contribute to it, but to say what is the one that this time was different that made--why it didn't catch fire earlier, I can't give you the answer.

**INTERVIEWER:** You don't make our job any easier (laughs).

**WARREN BUFFETT:** (Laughs) No, well, no, listen, I don't have a great answer. I'd probably have written an essay or something on it by this point. I mean, you know, I think it's going to defy an answer, to be perfectly honest. That doesn't mean that your time is wasted or anything. Understanding, you know, the pathology of bubbles is not an unimportant--we had one that was more severe. In fact, there was an article in the Omaha World Herald about three months ago that described how it was more severe; we had a bubble in the Midwest in the early '80s in farmland that created much more financial dislocation, but it was more limited to the farm belt than this particular bubble has, which has not hit as hard in terms of housing in the Midwest. So Nebraska was much harder hit in the farmland bubble. And the farmland bubble had the same logic to it. Inflation was out of control; Volcker hadn't really come in with his--with his meat axe to the economy, and people said, you know, you're not making more farmland, there are going to be more people eating, farmland gets more productive by the years, we learn more about it, fertilizers and all that sort of thing. And cash is trash, so you should go to and own something real, which was a farm. And I bought a farm from the FDIC, and well, no, it was the FDIC I think. They took over a bank 30 miles from here. I bought up a farm for $600 an acre that the bank had lent $2,000 an acre against. And the farm didn't know what I'd paid for it or the other guy had paid on it. And that farm had a productive capacity of probably $60 an acre in terms of what corn soybeans were selling for. To lend $2,000 against it when interest rates were 10% was madness. And both the banks in [unintelligible] and Nebraska went broke because they went insane. They got through the '30s all right, but the psychology that farms could do nothing but go up took over. And that was a significant but very miniature version of what could happen with houses countrywide.

**INTERVIEWER:** Now earlier you referenced the GSE, and it's been reported that in 2000 you sold nearly all of your Freddie Mac and Fannie Mae shares. What persuaded you in 2000 to think that those were no longer good investments?

**WARREN BUFFETT:** Well, I didn't know that they were not going to be good investments. But I was concerned about the management at both Freddie Mac and Fannie Mae, although our holdings were concentrated in Freddie Mac. They were trying to and proclaiming that they could increase earnings per share in some low double-digit range or something of the sort. And any time a large financial institution starts promising regular earnings increases you're going to have trouble. It isn't given to man to be able to run a financial institution where different interest rates scenarios will prevail and all of that comes to produce smooth regular earnings from a very large base to start with. So if people are thinking that way, they're going to do things maybe in accounting – it's turned out to be the case in both Freddie and Fannie – but also in operations that I would regard as unsound. I don't know when it'll happen, I don't even know for sure if it'll happen. It will happen eventually if they keep up that policy, and so we, or I, just decided to get out.

**INTERVIEWER:** The Washington Post reported on October 31, 2007 that you had provided some testimony the day before in a case against Freddie Mac's CEO where you had indicated that you became troubled when Freddie Mac made an investment unrelated to its mission. And you were quoted in that article as saying that you didn't think that it made any sense at all and you were concerned about what they might be doing that I didn't know about. What was that investment unrelated to its mission?

**WARREN BUFFETT:** As I remember, it was Philip Morris bonds, I think – I could be wrong, it might be R.J. Reynolds or something. But they'd made a large investment in that. Now they're dealing essentially with government guaranteed credit. We knew that then, we've had it ratified subsequently by what's happened. So here was an institution that was trying to serve two masters: Wall Street and her investors, and Congress. And they were using this power to do something that was totally unrelated to the mission; and then they gave me some half-baked explanation about how it increased liquidity which was just nonsense. And the truth was they were arbitraging the government's credit, and for something the government really didn't intend for them to do. And you know, there's seldom just one cockroach in the kitchen, you know. You turn on the light and all those others all start scurrying around. And I wasn't, I couldn't find the light switch, but I'd seen one.

**INTERVIEWER:** Shifting to more recent times. You've made investments in Goldman Sachs in September of 2008 and in General Electric. What were your considerations when you made those investments and were you persuaded by any government official to make those investments?

**WARREN BUFFETT:** I wasn't persuaded by--I was--in my own mind, there was only one way both the financial world and the economy was going to come out of this situation, that of paralysis in September of 2008, and I made the fundamental decision that we had really the right people in Bernanke and Paulson and in there with the President would back them up, that we had a government that would take the action that only the government could. It would take the action to get an economic machine that had become stalled basically back into action. And I didn't know what they would do; I didn't know what Congress would do. It didn't really make much difference. The important thing was the American public would come to believe that our government would do whatever it took. And I felt it would, it would have been suicide not to. But it hadn't been done in the early '30s, and therefore those companies like General Electric or Goldman Sachs were going to be fine over time. But it was a bet, essentially, on the fact that the government would not really shirk its responsibility at a time like that to leverage up when the rest of the world was trying to de-leverage and panicked.

**INTERVIEWER:** Around that same time on, October 17, 2008, you wrote an op-ed piece in the New York Times on why you were buying American stocks. And did anyone from the federal government or Federal Reserve ask you to write that?

**WARREN BUFFETT:** No, no.

**INTERVIEWER:** And similarly, I know you weren't persuaded by anything the government asked you to do, but did anyone ask you to make any investments in financial companies such as Goldman?

**WARREN BUFFETT:** No. Well, Goldman asked me to and GE asked me to and a number of other companies asked me to, but nobody from government.

**INTERVIEWER:** No one from government?

**WARREN BUFFETT:** No. I have--I have actually testified that in the connection with Lehman was trying to raise some money in the spring of 2008, and Dick Fuld was calling me, and he did get Hank Paulson to call but Hank did not urge me to buy. He was responding to the entreaties of Fuld that he make a call, but I was not asked to buy anything. Wouldn't have done any good if they'd asked (laughs)...

**INTERVIEWER:** Do you believe that your prominence as an investor and your stock purchases could alleviate the financial crisis, was that--?

**WARREN BUFFETT:** That was not a motivation.

**INTERVIEWER:** Was that a consideration?

**WARREN BUFFETT:** No, no, not a bit (laughs). My public spirit has stopped short of $8 billion.

**INTERVIEWER:** Would the American economy have been better off in the long run if there'd had been no exceptional government assistance to financial institutions? In other words, do you think that we've increased the likelihood of moral hazard in the long run?

**WARREN BUFFETT:** I think the moral hazard thing is misunderstood in a big way. There is no moral hazard existing with shareholders of Citigroup with Freddie Mac, with Fannie Mae, with WaMu, with Wachovia; you just go up and down the line. I mean, those people lost anywhere from 90% to 100% of their money. And the idea that they would walk away and think, ah, I've been saved by the federal government...when I think of just the companies I named, there's at least a half a trillion dollars of loss that the common share-holders now--there's another question with managements, which we might get into later. But in terms of moral hazard, I don't even un-derstand why people talk about that in terms of equity holdings.

**INTERVIEWER:** Do you think we would have been better off, though, if we had not the infusion of government assistance?

**WARREN BUFFETT:** I think it would be a disaster, you know. It would have. It would have been the disaster of all time.

**INTERVIEWER:** I'd like for you to try to help me square something you've been quot-ed as saying about credit default swaps, and I'm sure my colleague, Chris Seifer, has been focusing in on these areas and he'll ask you additional questions. But you've been quoted as saying credit default swaps were financial weapons of mass destruction.

**WARREN BUFFETT:** Well, I, I --no, I said derivatives.

**INTERVIEWER:** Derivatives, excuse me.

**WARREN BUFFETT:** Yeah, were financial--systemically they represented potential financial weapons of mass destruction. And I think-- I don't think there's any question about that.

**INTERVIEWER:** And in 2008 you began to invest in credit default swaps and I understand that–

**WARREN BUFFETT:** Yeah, we've sold insurance for a lot of years and sometimes that's credit insurance. And you know, I don't think the way--I don't see a connection between selling insurance and thinking something can be systemically dangerous – if, again, carried to extremes in terms of the leverage produced and the scope of contracts entered in – but I don't see anything improper about credit insurance. Banks have been doing that for decades with letters of credit and that sort of thing.

**INTERVIEWER:** And in terms of, though, your concern with derivatives, is it a question of the type of product or is it a question of the use or both?

**WARREN BUFFETT:** It's a question of being--it's the ability to inject enormous amounts of leverage into a system where leverage is dangerous, and without people fully appreciating the amount of leverage, and as a handmaiden of leverage, a risk of counterparties running up huge amounts of receivables and payables. And one of the reasons stock markets work well is that you've got a three-day settlement period. But if you have a one-year settlement period – in fact, I think over in Kuwait they did some years ago, and they had a total debacle – you would have far more problems. Well, derivatives and bonds havee very, very long settlement periods and things can happen between when you write a contract and if you have a settlement period. There was one at Gen Re that was 100 years, very hard to predict the behavior of somebody else 100 years from now (laughs). And derivatives present big problems.

Now, if there's only a small amount in use, it doesn't make that much difference to the system. But if they become more and more pervasive, more and more imaginative and less and in effect very little attention being paid to them, which is why I sounded a warning. I don't think they're evil per se, it's just they--I mean, there's nothing wrong with having a futures contract or something of the sort, but they do let people engage in massive mischief.

And the thing I found really extraordinary –
and Tracy, you might give them that letter – I
mean, I wrote this letter in 1982, about the
date--the, here, you've got a Commission
that's doing what before I did, you know,
many years ago. And when we had those
hearings after '29 we decided leverage was
dangerous for people and it could cause systemic problems when used in the stock market. And we had the Federal Reserve power
to determine margin requirements. We said
that was important and that if people got over
leveraged in the stocks they could cause a
problem not only for themselves but for others if it was done on a wide scale. And then we
came along in 1982 and we in a sense opened
up leverage to anybody in extreme measures;
and since that time, 28 years since then, I and
perhaps others, but I know I pointed out at
least 20 times, the real nonsense of saying
somebody at the Federal Reserves telling people they can only borrow 50% against stocks
or whatever the margin requirements have
been at various times. And then at the same
time telling them that you can go gamble, you
know, in S&P futures or something, the 2% or
3% margin or whatever it might be. And to
this day – and I've talked to Congress about
it – and to this day we sit there with a system
where the Federal Reserve is telling you how

much you can borrow against stocks, and we've got this parallel system where people can gamble anything they want virtually in terms of the most obvious one being the S&P futures. And I've seen no attempt by anybody to address that total contradiction – might be a suggestion for your commission.

**INTERVIEWER:** On that vein, we've been charged with talking about excess risk and excess speculation, and I know you've commented on what you view as speculation in one of your letters. But we've had some internal conversations within the commission itself about the use of the term speculation, whether it's a–

**WARREN BUFFETT:** It's an interesting – defining investment, speculation, and gambling is an interesting question.

**INTERVIEWER:** I'd be interested in, you know, what you think speculation is as opposed to investing, which you've written about, and also what you think excess speculation or excess risk is in that context.

**WARREN BUFFETT:** It's a tricky definition, you know, it's like pornography (laughs), the famous quote and all that, but I look at it in terms of the intent of the person engaging in the transaction. And an investment operation – and that's not the way Graham defines it in his book – but an investment operation in my view is one where you look to the asset itself to determine your decision to lay out some money now to get some more money back later on. So you look to the apartment house, you look to the stock, you look to the farm in terms of what that will produce. And you don't really care whether there's a quote under it all. You are basically committing some funds now to get more funds later on through the operation of the asset.

Speculation, I would define as much more focused on the price action of the stock, particularly that you buy or the indexed future or something of the sort. Because you are not really--you are counting on, for whatever factors – could be quarterly earnings, could be up or it's going to split or whatever it may be, or increase the dividend – but you are not looking to the asset itself. And I say the real test of how you, what you're doing is whether you care whether the markets are open. When I buy a stock, I don't care whether they close the stock market tomorrow for a couple of years because I'm looking to the business – Coca-Cola or whatever it may be – to produce returns for me in the future from the business. Now if I care whether the stock market is open tomorrow, then I say to some extent I'm speculating because I'm thinking about whether the price is going to go up tomorrow or not. I don't know where the price is going to go.

And then gambling I would define as engaging in a transaction which doesn't need to be part of the system. I mean, if I want to bet on a football game, you know, the football game's operation is not dependent on whether I bet or not. Now, if I want to bet on October wheat or something of the sort, people have to raise wheat, and when they plant it they don't know what the price is going be later on. So you need activity on the other side of that and who may be speculating on it, but it is not an artificial transaction that has no necessity for existing in an economic framework. And the gambling propensity with people is huge. I mean, you took a--you know, some terrible sand out in the west about 100 years ago and you created, you know, huge industry with people flying thousands of miles to do things which are mathematically unintelligent, you know. Now that shows something in mankind that has a strong, strong behavioral--has a strong behavioral aspect to it. And think how much easier it is, you know, to sit there in front of a computer and have the same amount of fun without, you know, getting on a plane and going a 1,000 miles and having to make reservations and do all that sort of thing. So with this propensity to gamble – encouraged, incidentally, by the state with lotteries, you know, with terrible odds attached to them – people don't have to be trained to want to gamble in this country, but they, they have this instinct, a great many people. They're encouraged when they see some successes around; that's why the bells and whistles go off in the casino when somebody hits a jackpot, you know.

So, you know, you have all these things pushing to that, including governmental urging to buy lottery tickets and all that sort of thing. And now you've got a vehicle like, you know, S&P futures or something where you can go in and out and where Congress has granted particularly favorable tax treatment to you if you win. I mean, you can be in for ten seconds and have 60% long-term gain, which I regard as, you know, extraordinary. But it exists. That's all I know about gambling, actually speculation (laughs), but I do know it when I see it.

**INTERVIEWER:** My last question before I turn things over is you've mentioned management, and people have observed that there have been failures of management at Wall Street banks. Similarly, people have described there to be failures of regulators during this crisis.

**WARREN BUFFETT:** Failures of the media, failures of, you know, Congress failures, you know. Commentators, you know.

**INTERVIEWER:** How did management fail and what do you view as the essential failures in management of the Wall Street firms, and similarly, what would you view as the failures of the regulators leading up to and during the crisis?

**WARREN BUFFETT:** Well, they didn't anticipate, you know, how extraordinary a bubble could be created, you know. And very difficult to fault them because so few people have a difficult time doing that when a crowd is rushing in one direction knowing the other direction is very hard. And usually the people that do that become discredited by the price action, you know. If you were a Cassandra in 2005 or 2006 and houses kept going up, you know, after a while people quit listening and it [unintelligible] because they're nuts anyway, you know, anything that's going on, so you, you have a fringe element to Cassandras too. Conceivably, you know, if the President of the United States, you know, or the Chairman of the Fed or somebody made a strong statement – Greenspan made a strong statement, I remember, in 1996, you know, about irrational consumers, you know, that didn't stop the stock market. When people think there's easy money available, they're not inclined to change. Particularly if somebody said a month or two ago, watch out for this easy money, and then their neighbors made some more money in the ensuing month or two – it's just, it's overwhelming. And we've seen it.

**INTERVIEWER:** And the failures of regulators? Were there any?

**WARREN BUFFETT:** Well, oh, I mean, there are failures of everybody in one sense. But the biggest failure is that we're unable to act contrary to the way humans act in these situations. I mean, it would have--you can say regulators should have been out there screaming about the fact you people are doing foolish things, and sure, regulators could have stopped it. If a regulator said, or Congress could have stopped – Freddie and Fannie, if Freddie and Fannie had said, you know, we will only accept mortgages with 30% down payments, verified income and the payments can't be more than 30% of your income, you know, that would have stopped it. But who, you know, who could do that?

**INTERVIEWER:** Do you think if Fannie–

**WARREN BUFFETT:** In fact, if I think you recommend that (laughs), of course, for future mortgage actions, you'd better get an unlisted phone number.

**INTERVIEWER:** (Laughs) Do you think if Fannie had tighter standards and tighter controls that we could have averted a financial crisis?

**WARREN BUFFETT:** Well, Freddie and Fannie were in a position--whether they were practically in that position, whether Congress, you know, would have tolerated them coming out with really much stricter standards, I don't think it probably could have happened. I'm not sure they wanted it to happen either. I mean, they were enjoying the party too. And they didn't think the party was going to end like this. I mean, it wasn't like somebody was thinking this is going to end in a paralysis of the American economy, you know. They just, they started believing what other people believed. It's very tough to fight that. We will have other bubbles in the future, I mean, there's no question about that. I don't think the President of the United States, you know, could have stopped it by rhetoric. And I think if any President of the United States had said, you know, I'm campaigning on a program of 30% down payments, verified income and not more than 30, you know, they might not have impeached him but they sure as hell wouldn't have re-elected him (laughs).

**INTERVIEWER:** Thanks. I'm going to primarily ask you about derivatives generally, but I want to ask you about a couple of things different first. In your most recent shareholder letter you talked about how Berkshire Hathaway – that Berkshire Hathaway would never become dependent on the kindness of strangers.

**WARREN BUFFETT:** Absolutely.

**INTERVIEWER:** And too big to fail was not a fallback position, and that the company would always have sufficient cash, apparently in the magnitude of $20 billion these days, so that would not be a problem. Generally, when you look at the issue of too big to fail, is it just a liquidity issue? Do you have enough cash? No one's too big to fail because the issue will never come up?

**WARREN BUFFETT:** You'll have the institutions too big to fail. We still have them now; I mean, we'll have them after. Your commission reports, certainly – I mean, Freddie and Fannie, we've totally acknowledged we got--and incidentally are too big to fail. I'm not quarrelling with the policy on it and they aren't too big to wipe out the shareholders though, I mean. So it isn't, you know, society has done the right thing with Freddie and Fannie, in my view. They've wiped out the shareholders; nobody's got any illusion that the government is protecting them as an equity holder. They do have the belief that they will be protected as debt holders but we were sending that message well before the bubble. I mean, you know, Congress would say technically we aren't backing them and they've only got this two and quarter million or whatever it was. But Freddie and Fannie paper was held all over the world, and you know, in a world where the other guy's got nuclear bombs (laughs), you're sort of implying to them that the government was standing behind this. I don't think you would have wanted to default on Freddie and Fannie, so I think we've done the right thing. But there will be institutions that are too big to fail but they're not too big to wipe out the shareholders, and I would argue that they're not too big to – I think there should be different incentives with institutions like that with the top, the top management. They're not too big to send away to the CEO that caused the problem, away without a dime.

**INTERVIEWER:** And I understand that is – I'm just asking if your opinion is the answer to the too-big-to-fail problem – make them hold more cash?

**WARREN BUFFETT:** The answer – and it isn't a perfect answer, you will always have institutions too big to fail and sometimes they will fail in the next 100 years. But you will have fewer failures if the person on top and the Board of Directors who select that person and who set the terms of his or her employment if they have a lot to lose. And in this particular incident the shareholders have got – probably it's well over half a trillion, maybe approaching a trillion; they've suffered the losses, society has suffered the losses from all the disruption in the second place. Directors and CEOs, CEOs, you know, they only have 80% of what they had before, but they're all wealthy beyond the dream of most Americans. The directors, you know, have collected their $200,000 or $300,000 a year and they're protected by insurance. And so the people that are in a position to make decisions day by day as to trading off the safety of the institution versus the chance for improving quarterly earnings or something of the sort, you need different incentives in my view. And so far nothing's been done on that.

**INTERVIEWER:** So let me ask you, because another area we look at for potential contributing costs of financial crisis are compensation structures and incentive structures within firms. And you have seen a lot of firms, you know, come out since the crisis and say, oh well, now we're doing things differently. Now we pay more of our executives in stock. Now the stock or cash bonuses are subject to claw back provisions and vesting periods or whatever. Do you have any thoughts on, you know, how you do make them have accountability for when things go wrong?

**WARREN BUFFETT:** Well, all of that is good. I mean, that's better than what existed before. But I think it has to be far more Draconian than that to really change behavior big time. And the difference is between a guy making $100 million and $50 million, you know, that, I don't think, or clawing back $25 million of it, sure, you know, it registers but it doesn't – I don't think it changes behavior that much compared to at least what I would have in mind.

**INTERVIEWER:** Do you – and the next

thing I was going to ask you – what are the more Draconian–

**WARREN BUFFETT:** I think it's enormously important when you get very big financial institutions and maybe in other cases too. Well, we're in a building run by the Keywood Company. It's the most successful construction company in the world and it has been for decades. Nobody's ever heard of it but it's huge and it's got a set of management principles and basically it started with Pete Keywood saying that arranging a compensation system so that the company got in trouble; not only he went broke but all the people that got him in trouble went broke. And you, when you have the ability to do things with government-guaranteed money as the banks or something, or Freddie and Fannie, whatever it may be, you need a person at the top who has all of the downside that somebody has that loses their job, you know, working in an auto factory or something of the sort. And that will change behavior.

Now you can argue it may make them too cautious, I mean that, so you want some upside for them, too, I mean, you want them to balance somehow their interest in a way that society might balance its interest. And as part of that, with the CEO, I think, you need important but far less Draconian arrangements in terms of directors. Because they can't evaluate risk in a large institution or have risk committees telling them what's going on. But they can set the terms of employment for the CEO in a way that will make him terribly risk-conscious, and if they don't do that, if they haven't done it effectively, I think there should be significant downside to them. I've suggested to them that maybe they give back five times the highest compensation they received in the previous five years or something. It has to be meaningful but it can't be so Draconian that you don't get directors. You'll get CEOs, you don't have to worry about that; if you've got a lot of upside for CEOs you can give them the downside of, you know, sack cloth and ashes, and you'll still get CEOs that–

**INTERVIEWER:** The downside, of course, is just zero because they file bankruptcy and that's it. I had a question for you, though, related to that: In the 50 years plus that you've been investing, have you seen changes in compensation approaches, policies, attitudes with respect to senior management at these various–

**WARREN BUFFETT:** Well, it's gradually, maybe not--yeah, it's changed over the years, and you've seen it just in the relationship of top management compensation to the average employee. So it has gotten considerably more generous, if you want to use that term, from 50 years ago. There used to be a few outstanding – Bethlehem Steel was famous for paying a lot of money, and you go way, way back and all that, but in general it wasn't expected. And there's some ironic aspects to that because in a sense the SEC has required more exposure in pay packages and everything like that, so you've got this envy factor. I mean, you know, the same thing that happens in baseball. I mean, if you bat .320 you expect to get more than .310, and nobody knows in business whether you're batting .320 or not, so everybody says they're a .320 hitter. And the Board of Directors has to say, well, we've got a .320 hitter because they couldn't be responsible for picking a guy that bats .250. So you have this racheting effect which I've talked about a lot of times. And the more information that's published about compensation, in a way, the worse it's gotten in terms of what people do. Because they look at the other guy and he's got personal use of the plane or whatever it may be (laughs) and that gets built into the next contract. So it's changed over the years, and the downside does not parallel the upside in terms of innovation.

**INTERVIEWER:** Well, let me ask you: other than looking at perhaps more Draconian measures for money and compensation that is received, do you have any opinions on just the amounts that are paid in whatever form in the first place? And for example, one of things we see – and frankly, I saw this before I came to the FCIC – is you always read in a proxy statement that all these companies go out and hire somebody to do a survey and see, you know, to come up with executive compensation, and they're looking at a bunch of companies that pay their executives a lot of money. And they say, okay, you should get a whole lot of money too.

**WARREN BUFFETT:** Ratchet, ratchet, ratchet, that's the name of the comp board.

**INTERVIEWER:** I mean, do you have any opinions on just the level of executive compensation?

**WARREN BUFFETT:** Well, it's perfectly understandable. I mean, you've got a CEO that cares enormously about his compensation. You've got a compensation committee that meets, you know, for a few hours maybe every meeting. You've got a human relations vice president who is working for the CEO that probably suggests a compensation consultant. But a compensation consultant who is Draconian is not going to get hired generally around, or even too innovative on the downside, there's just--so it is, you know, it's the agency problem that the economist would call it. But it's very--it's very hard over time, and then you've got this comparison factor which embodies all the other things I just mentioned, and then they get into the system and people say, well, we didn't hire a guy in the bottom quartile to be our CEO so we're not going to compare to the bottom quartile, we're not getting compared to the next to bottom quartile. So it just ratchets up and we've seen it. And I am the comp committee for 70-some companies which Berkshire owns. It's not rocket science. And we pay a lot of money to some of our CEOs but it's all performance. When they make a lot of money it's performance related. And we have different arrangements for different people. But we've never hired a compensation consultant, ever. And we never will. I mean, if I don't know enough to figure out the compensation for these people, you know, somebody else should be in my job. And the test is how do they perform and do they leave for other places and, you know, we've got the record on that. The problem, you know, I'm in a position of control, I am the stockholder of these subsidiary companies and when you get people in between who are getting paid, you know, $200,000 to $300,000 a year being on a Board which is important to some of them and where they're hoping that they get put on some other Board so they've got another $200,000$300,000 a year, they are not exactly going to be doberman pinschers, you know, in policing things.

**INTERVIEWER:** In terms of, we've seen Bear fail, Lehman fail, Merrill essentially fail and get acquired by BofA and Morgan Stanley and Goldman both received government assistance and Goldman received the benefit of your investment too. All of those investment banking franchises, I believe the compensation structure was essentially minimum 45% of net revenues was getting paid out in comp, some years even higher. Any opinion on that structure?

**WARREN BUFFETT:** I can tell you it's very hard to change. I was at Solomon (laughs) and it, the nature of Wall Street is that overall it makes a lot of money relative to the number of people involved, relative to the IQ of the people involved and relative to the energy expended. They work hard, they're bright, but they aren't, they don't work that much harder or that much brighter than somebody that, you know, is building a dam someplace, you know, or a whole lot of other jobs. But in a market system it pays off very, very big, you know. And it, in effect, you know, boxing pays off very big now compared to what it did when the only auditorium we had was 25,000 seats at Madison Square Garden and now you've cable television so you can put a couple of, you know, lightweights who you'll never of again, you know, on pay per view and they'll get millions for it now. Market systems produce strange results and Wall Street, in general, the capital markets are so big, there's so much money, taking a small percentage results in a huge amount of money per capita in terms of the people that work in it. And they're not inclined to give it up.

**INTERVIEWER:** When you see the general compensation structure in terms of percentage payout and the types of structures they have with ever different levels of Draconian claw backs or whatever and the risks that were taken that resulted in failures and bailouts, I mean, do you see in the big, you know, the compensation picture in general as a contributing cause or part of the story of what happened on the street?

**WARREN BUFFETT:** Comp, most of the comp, you're talking about individual trader or something, you know, and they have, you know, they call it trader's option. That they've got the upside, they have a good year and they have a bad year, you know. They might not have a good year again next year, they might go to a different firm but they really, their interests are not totally aligned with shareholders. And I would say this, I think most managements of Wall Street firms and I was around Solomon and I know what happens at [unintelligible], they're trying, they want to align them, I mean, it isn't, you know, it isn't like the top management is oblivious to this problem. But I can just tell you, being at Solomon personally, it's just, it's a real problem because the fellow can go next door or he can set up a hedge fund or whatever it may be. You don't, you don't have a good way of having some guy that produces x dollars of revenues to give him 10% of x because he'll figure out, he'll find some other place that will give him 20% of x or whatever it may be. It is a tough managerial problem, but I think the best thing again, if you're worrying about the Bear Stearnses of the world or anything is to have an arrangement in place that if they ever have to go to the federal government for help that the CEO and his spouse come away with nothing. And I think that can be done. And I think if society is required to step in and, you know, come up with all kinds of things, disrupt, you know, the lives of millions of Americans in various ways, I think there ought to be a lot of downside. And I think that would change behavior more than any, trying to write some terribly complicated thing, you know, that only 38% of us can (laughs). I just don't know how to write rules otherwise. This would get their attention and I wouldn't try to, I wouldn't know how to get more specific than that.

**INTERVIEWER:** Well, then, let me ask you this then. If the CEOs and their spouse--unlucky marriage there--you know, have to give back everything-

**WARREN BUFFETT:** You'd think the spouse would be a better police than the regulator (laughs)

**INTERVIEWER:** You know, that they need to give everything back or be shown the door, if the company needs government assistance, there are CEOs at some firms that got government assistance that are still there including for example Mr. Blankfein that I've at least read you said, boy, if they're going to replace Blankfein I'd like to replace them with his brother.

**WARREN BUFFETT:** Yeah, I don't think they needed assistance. The system needed assistance then but if, when they had that famous meeting at the treasury on Monday if they hadn't called on Goldman Sachs and they called on the others, Goldman would have been fine. The system needed to be supported, just, you know, it wasn't important the precise action. It was that the world had to see that the federal government was going to do whatever it took. And nobody knew whatever it took meant. But they did need to see conviction, action and all of that. And Bernanke and Paulson they could have called on nine different other institutions, these were particularly good names to have there, but had gone through the same mechanism and Goldman Sachs would have been fine, Wells Fargo would have been fine. They didn't need the money, the system needed the reassurance that the government was going to act.

**INTERVIEWER:** It's, we've been reported when you made the investment in Goldman in September of '08 that you were, you know, somewhat betting on the government taking some type of action.

**WARREN BUFFETT:** Not in relation to Goldman though, but in the, no, I was betting on the fact the federal government would show the will to the American people that they would, in effect, do whatever it took to re-start the engine.

**INTERVIEWER:** So, I don't know if you can answer this question because it's somewhat of a hypothetical but if you knew then that the government was not going to put any money into Goldman would you have still made the investment?

**WARREN BUFFETT:** Oh, yeah, it wouldn't bother me whether I'm going to put it in Goldman but if I thought the government was not going to reassure the American public through acts, speeches whatever it might be that they were going to do whatever it took to save the system, I would have, you know, got my mattress out. But, Goldman did not need the money, the system needed the reassurance. But Goldman would have been, if they'd ever been called down there they would have been fine. I wouldn't have put the money in if I thought Goldman needed specific government action. But I also would not have put the money in if I thought the government was going to stand by and watch things unfold.

**INTERVIEWER:** Okay. So now let's actually turn to derivatives, I didn't think we'd spend that much time--the statute amongst other things tells us to look at the role of derivatives that it played in the financial crisis and we have been talking to "many" experts in the field that, whether they're academicians or market participants that work with derivatives. And, of course, we've read, you know, what you've written in the shareholder letters, the weapons of mass destruction, they can lead to excess risk and leverage and there's counterparty risk. At the same time if they're managed effectively they can be fine although I think in your shareholder letters you're primarily talking about credit derivatives there but I may be mistaken.

**WARREN BUFFETT:** Well, when we buy the Burlington Northern, they're hedging diesel fuel. Now what I tell them is I wouldn't do it if I were them but it's entirely up to them. I mean, diesel fuel's a big cost for them and they've got pass-through costs to some of the people that use the railroad and they don't have passthroughs so they're exposed partly. The only, I tell them if they really don't want diesel fuel on the market we'll just close up the railroad and then all trade diesel fuel all day, you know. And if they don't know it, they're going to be out the frictional costs over time. The reason many of them do it is that they want, the public companies, they want to smooth earnings. And I'm not saying there's anything wrong with that but that is the motivation. They're not going to, they're going to lose as much on the diesel fuel contracts over time as they make but they can protect themselves just like Coca-Cola does on foreign exchange and they make a big thing of this. I wouldn't do it, they do, but all kinds, most companies what to do that. Anheuser-Busch was just talking about it in Business Week a few weeks ago how they do it. It's a common practice. It's overdone in my view, but it is the response to the fact that the market doesn't like the fact that diesel fuel could affect the earnings of Burlington or Union Pacific up and down in some quarter when really over time they're not going to make any, you know, they're not going to save any money by doing it in my view.

**INTERVIEWER:** And just broadly, whether it's interest rate, foreign exchange commodity equities or credit derivatives, do you have a view on whether they contributed or caused the financial crisis, what role they played whether it was a cause, a contributing cause, a propagating mechanism or anything?

**WARREN BUFFETT:** Anything that increased leverage significantly tends to make, it can't even create a crisis, but it would tend to accentuate any crisis that occurs. So I think that if Lehman had been less leveraged there would have been less problems in the way of problems. And part of that leverage arose from the use of derivatives. And part of the dislocation that took place afterwards arose from that. And there's some interesting material if you look at, I don't exactly what Lehman material I was looking at, but they had a netting arrangement with the Bank of America as I remember and, you know, the day before they went broke and these are very, very, very rough figures from memory, but as I remember the day before they went broke Bank of America was in a minus position of $600 million or something like that they had deposited which I think J.P. Morgan in relation to Lehman and I think that the day they went broke it reversed to a billion and a half in the other direction and those are big numbers. And I think the numbers are, I think I'm right on just order of magnitude. So when things like that exist in the system, you know, that's under stress for other reasons, it becomes a magnifying factor. How big of one you don't know. But Lehman would have had less impact on the system if they had not had the derivative book they had. Now they had plenty of bad real estate investments and a whole bunch of other things as well.

**INTERVIEWER:** And when you talk about the leverage and the counterparty risk from derivatives are you talking about certain types or derivatives, you know, there's the five categories we see. Do you have any opinion on--?

**WARREN BUFFETT:** Unfortunately, yeah, unfortunately people were not really imaginative about derivatives. I mean it started out with the simple ones, you know, interest rates, swaps and that sort of thing, foreign currency. And then the profit got driven away from those. When I was at Solomon they talked about in the plain vanilla contracts there wasn't any money in it anymore because they were on the screens and everybody knew-- but what they call sometimes the toxic waste, there was a lot of money in and, you know, the more complicated the derivative, well, you remember the situation with Proctor and Gamble thing from the Banker's Trust and American Greetings and all of that, if you read the nature of those contracts where they had these exploding factors, you know, when you got beyond a certain point, the CFO of a place like Proctor and Gamble or American Greetings was probably not understanding those things very well. And there's just more money in contracts that people don't understand. And so they get this proliferation of these things and who knows what's in the mind of the end user of the things that, you know, they're protecting themselves against the sort of Jefferson County in Alabama and all kinds of things. So, you know, it's, it's an instrument that's prone to lots of mischief because long settlement periods, complicated formulas for sometimes deriving the variables that are entering into the eventual payout, it's got a lot of possibilities for mischief. And a lot's been caused. And mischief doesn't make much difference if it's, you know, one guy, you know, rolling dice against another and one guy's loaded a dice they're doing for $5 a throw but it makes a lot of difference when you get into big numbers.

**INTERVIEWER:** So let me ask you on the issue of transparency you wrote in your shareholder letter, not the recent one, but the one from the year before that it's simply impossible for investors to understand and analyze these. It was impossible or at least very difficult for auditors to audit them and for regulators to regulate them and after spending time with financial institutions 10K or whatever else you reached for a bottle of aspirin which I can very much appreciate. (laughter) But, and you also wrote, you know, that policymakers talk about transparency as being a great cure-all for-

**WARREN BUFFETT:** It's a great word (laughs).

**WARREN BUFFETT:** Nobody can be against transparency.

**INTERVIEWER:** But, you said, you know, look, I don't know of any reporting system, you know, that can fix this. So, I mean, obviously, you know, we're not just looking at causes of the financial crisis but this whole lack of transparency particularly in the area of derivatives as you know from taking aspirin for your headaches after looking at 10Ks, is a problem. So I'm just wondering what, you know, your opinions are and how do we address that problem?

**WARREN BUFFETT:** I think it's a terribly difficult problem, well, it was so difficult a problem I didn't think I could solve it. We bought Gen Re which had 23,000 derivative contracts. I could have hired 15 of the smartest people that, you know, math majors, PhDs and I could have given them carte blanche to devise any reporting system to me that would enable me to get my mind around what exposure that I had and it wouldn't have worked. I mean, it just, the only answer was to get out of it. Can you imagine 23,000 contracts with 900 institutions all over the world with probably

200 of them names I can't pronounce. And all of these contracts extending years into the future, multiple variables, you know, and all of these, you can't manage it. In my view, I wouldn't be able to manage something like that. And if I read a 10K that's 300 pages long and it describes notional values of all this, not to impugn anybody because probably one of the best managed really large institutions around, but if I look at J.P. Morgan I see two trillion in receivables, two trillion in payables, a trillion and seven netted off on each side of the 300 billion remaining maybe 200 billion collateralized. But that's all fine but I don't know what dis-continuities are going to do to those numbers overnight if there's a, if there's a major nuclear, chemical or biological terrorist action that really is disruptive to the whole financial system here, who the hell knows what happens to those numbers on both sides or thousands of counterparties around. So I don't think it's -- I think it's virtually unmanageable.

**WARREN BUFFETT:** Certainly it is, would be for me.

**INTERVIEWER:** And let me ask, well, Goldman's the K, I looked at recently and there I see over a million contracts.

**WARREN BUFFETT:** Over a million contracts

**INTERVIEWER:** They don't disclose notional values in the K, at least not that I found yet, but, you know, they do disclose when you take out the netting, it's about one and a half trillion dollars both assets and liabilities go to BIS and get information from Goldman, it's not in their 10K, it's like 45 trillion when you add up all the numbers.

**WARREN BUFFETT:** Its bigger at J.P. Morgan. (laughs)

**INTERVIEWER:** And I don't see anything in the Ks and there is a question coming, I promise, (laughs) on who the counterparties are. So, I mean, does, would that help in transparency, some more disclosure on who the counterparties are?

**WARREN BUFFETT:** You can't design the system, I don't believe, I mean, I couldn't design the system and I've got a smart partner, Charlie Munger and we, the two of us couldn't design a system or come close to designing a system that would have told us what we were doing. So we got out. And we do know what we're doing with the 250 contracts we've got. And frankly I think we do a better job of disclosure of our derivatives position than any company in the United States, you know. We just tell people what we've done but, that's easy to do with 250 contracts or thereabouts and they only fall into a couple of categories. But I want to know, I want to know every contract and I can do that with the way we've done it. But I can't do it with 23,000 that a bunch of traders are putting on. I'm putting these on myself and I really only about two or three decisions that go through my mind in doing that. But to have a group of traders putting on thousands of them and counting on the behavior of party A over here to be the offset to what might happen with party C and I'm in between, I just, I don't know how to do that. And I don't think really anybody knows how to do that. And I probably shouldn't talk about names on this but I've had discussions with very important people about this in the past before the crisis hit and those people were confident that risk committees could come in with spreadsheets and explain it all and I always thought that was total nonsense.

**INTERVIEWER:** There's at least been some recent reports in the press that you've been lobbying against the retroactive, adjustment of the retroactive effect or at least some provisions in legislation that would require collateral to be-

**WARREN BUFFETT:** Yeah, we're not against collateral being required at all as far as--we do say if you're changing contracts retroactively that if a change in any part of the contract is made that the party benefiting from that change should pay the appropriate amount to the party that's suffering from it. Now when we put on our contracts because we didn't want to get ourselves in a position where we were a problem to the country, we negotiated for non-collateral type contracts. Now the price of collateralized contracts we would have received considerably more in the way of premiums if we had agreed to collateral. Right now we're looking at one contract where we can get paid $11 million if we agree to put up collateral and we can get paid $7.5 million if we don't agree to put up collateral. Every other term of the contract is the same. So all we say is if these things are changed retroactively, we want to be paid for the difference in value between a collateralized contract and a non-collateralized contract. And otherwise, incidentally it isn't just us, Coca-Cola, Anheuser-Busch, you name it, will have to send money to Wall Street as part of the deal that will be changed from before. And there's nothing wrong with that, if it's a

matter of public policy that they want all contracts collateralized including changing them retroactively. There may be a constitutional problem, I'm not sure about that. But if the difference was paid for the difference between a value of the collateralized contract we were over $150 million on, during the height of the crisis on just a relatively small piece of it. If we would accept, if we would change from non-collateralized contract to a collateralized contract, my Wall Street, big Wall Street firm and we just say if that's forced upon us to do that we want $150 million or whatever the appropriate number is. We sold a house in effect that was unfurnished and if we sold it furnished we would have gotten more money and if the government says now later on, two years after we made the deal, you've got to give the furniture too we want to get paid. And I think that would probably stand up in court incidentally, I mean, if it wasn't even addressed in the bill. But we'll see what happens on-

**INTERVIEWER:** Sure. Other things we've heard from other folks that I'll ask your opinion on, a lot of people seem to think a lot of over the counter derivatives are really pretty standardized contracts that should be triggered on an exchange. Any opinions on that?

**WARREN BUFFETT:** Well, I think it's very hard to do. I mean, you've got right now certain foreign exchange contracts that are traded on exchanges. The volume is practically nothing. Because there, let's just take a Swiss Franc contract. There's a September contract and a December contract and a March contract. But if we want to hedge some instrument we've got and we've done this with a few contracts, we want to hedge some contract that comes due December 16th, we probably want to have a contract, a forward contract expires December 16th. And so whereas it's easy to have and I don't know whether July corn or October corn of whatever it may be there's not a big delivery, there's not a big tailoring of the specific industry's requirements. You can get away with four different expiration dates or S&P

you can get away with four expiration dates or something but if you've got a power contract or something of the sort, to deliver electricity on July 15th and you worry about what you might have to buy in the merchant market to do it you're probably going to need one that contracted July 15th. And I don't know how you standardize, I mean, it's very easy to have standardized October copper and oil, I mean, you know, you got oil contracts extending out for many years or natural gas, but they are just periodic settlement dates. And I think that gets, that gets very tough with a great many derivative contracts. But I don't, I'm no expert on how all this works, I mean, there may be ways of solving that in terms of exchanges.

**INTERVIEWER:** Let me ask you about regulation. One of the things that we know from doing some research is that, of course, back in the beginning of the decade or the beginning of 2000 was the Commodities Futures Modernization Act, that had terms in it that said you can't regulate credit derivatives. So they went unregulated. Any opinions on regulation of credit derivatives or derivatives in general?

**WARREN BUFFETT:** I think it's very tough to do and I will tell you that whenever I hear the terms modernization or innovation in financial markets, I reach for my wallet (laughs). It's, usually what they mean is revenue producing and I think it's very tough. I mean that's what I got into in my letter of 1982, I mean, you are opening Pandora's box when you give people the right to either invest, speculate or gamble on very long term contracts, you know, with minimal margin requirements and all. I mean, it can pose dangers to the system but it gets down to leverage overall. I mean, if you don't have leverage, you don't get into trouble. That's the only way a smart person can go broke (laughs). And I've always said if you're smart you don't need it and if you're dumb you shouldn't be using it. So I'm not a big fan of leverage. But leverage and incentives are in my view things that, try to focus on. And recognizing that there's a lot of limitations on what you can do. But if, I mean, we've always felt that way with banks. The bank has the right to use government guaranteed money in effect. You've got to have some limitations on leverage so then they come up with SIVs and derivatives and all kinds of ways to increase leverage without breaking the rules. And then, it's a tough question but I would be fairly tough about how I would go at that. And I don't like to keep going back to it but I, it doesn't seem to be anything talked about much, but the CEO is the guy making the decisions, I'm making the decisions at Berkshire. When I make the decisions at Berkshire, I'm thinking about the fact that a) I've got 99% of my net worth in it and it's all going to charities so I mean, if I cause this place to go broke, there's a lot of downside to me. And there's a lot of downside to the Keywood Company if they do silly things in their construction business. And I think that downside has an effect on people.

**INTERVIEWER:** Well, do you think that, I mean, you keep coming back to the CEO and accountability for perhaps unreasonable risks they are taking. Is that an area that you think regulation should address?

**WARREN BUFFETT:** Yeah, I think, but, you know, I've never written a Bill in my life so I don't know how you do that. But I do think that if I were in charge I would have some, yeah, I would, wouldn't have to be very complicated. I mean, we're not talking about some small community bank or anything. We're talking about institutions that require government intervention. The FDIC will take care of the small banks and all that. I mean, a lot of those will be a lot of personal ownership anyway. But FDIC is not the federal government. I mean, that is banks paying for banks errors but when society, the U.S. government starts paying for specific errors that-I think there ought to be a lot of downside.

**INTERVIEWER:** Can I follow up on that. You mentioned small banks and community banks. We've read stories and certainly heard reports about community banks investing in CDOs investing in-

**WARREN BUFFETT:** They bought a lot of

Freddie and Fannie preferreds, a lot of money lost in that.

**INTERVIEWER:** Correct, correct. But with respect to CDOs and many of them bought what were rated as triple A tranches of CDOs. Over 90% of the ratings on CDOs have been downgraded to near or around junk status. How much, putting aside legal responsibility because credit rating agencies have asserted they have a First Amendment right, how much though responsibility in the moral sense or otherwise do credit rating agencies have for the decisions by the investment community to rely on their ratings, that triple A meant triple A. How much responsibility do you think the credit rating agencies have for these decisions that the community banks made and subsequently made to their demise?

**WARREN BUFFETT:** What do you think if you're a banker? Your job is to assess the credit of whatever you're committing to. And the interesting thing about those CDOs and a lot of them consisted of hybrid bank securities. I mean, so they were actually benefiting and there were a lot of hybrid bank securities put in the CDOs and they were benefiting from raising money from that forum. And that turned out to be a way poorer asset than they thought. They created the liability to some degree as they grew. But I would get back to the fact that if you run a bank, you know, I think your job is to assess the credit of when you lay out money whether you're buying U.S. treasuries, whether you're bonds of Greece, whether you're buying or lending money to, for construction and, I think I would not want to cop out really, I was relying on a rating agency. And the rating agencies they have models and we all have models in our mind, you know, when we're investing but they've got them all worked out, you know, with a lot of checklists and all of that sort of thing. I don't believe in those myself, only to say I've got a model in my mind, everybody has a model in their mind when they're making investments. But reliance on models, you know, work 98% of the time but it's, they never work 100% of the time. And everybody ought to realize that that's using them.

**INTERVIEWER:** You mentioned transparency earlier as well. These CDO instruments were largely opaque in terms of compositions and the like to the investors who were investing in them. They were structured and created though around the ratings and in connection with the ratings and the rating agencies. Do you think, though, that because of the opaqueness of these instruments rat-ings became in the minds of investors more important than perhaps maybe they should have been?

**WARREN BUFFETT:** Well, I would say that, you know, anybody that's investing in some-thing they consider opaque should just walk away. I mean, whether it's a common stock or, you know, new invention or whatever it may be. You know, that's why Graham wrote books is to try and get people to, you know, invest, to take that investment, it's very tough to get that message across. And you'd think bankers however would have learned by the time they get to run a bank.

**INTERVIEWER:** Okay. Let's move away from derivatives now and talk about, I mean, we talked about several areas already today about your views on causes or contributing causes to the financial crisis. Of course we have a statute with a gazillion things in there telling us to investigate and I know time's probably starting to run short so I'd like to first just ask you, you know, what haven't you told us in terms of do you think were, you know, important contributing causes of the crisis. And then I'm going to try to quickly go down the list in our statute and get your ideas on this.

**WARREN BUFFETT:** Well, I think the primary cause was a almost universal belief among everybody, and I don't ascribe particular blame to any part of it, but it's Congress, media, regulators, home owners, mortgage bankers, Wall Street, everybody that house prices would go up. And you apply that to a 22 trillion dollar asset class that's leveraged up in many cases and when that goes wrong you're going to have all kinds of consequences and it's going to hit not only the people that did the unsound things but to some extent the people that did the semi-sound and then finally the sound things even if it is allowed to gather enough momentum of its own on the downside, the same kind of momentum it had on the upside. I think contributing to that, causing the bubble to pop even louder was and maybe even to blow it up some was improper incentive systems and leverage. I mean, those--but they will contribute to almost any bubble that you have whether it's the internet or anything else. Incentive systems during the internet were terrible. I mean, you just, you formed a company and you said I'm going to somehow deliver a billion eyeballs and somebody said well, that's $50 a piece or something. I mean, you get craziness that goes on there. Leverage was not as much a factor in the internet bubble but I think in this particular bubble because leverage is part of, so much a part of real estate that once you loosen up on that, you provide fuel because that bubble will get even bigger and you made the pop even bigger when it finally did pop.

**INTERVIEWER:** Any views on the role of fraud, whether mortgage fraud or other types of fraud in the crisis?

**WARREN BUFFETT:** No, I mean, it was obviously a lot of fraud. There was fraud on the parts of the borrowers and there were frauds on part of the intermediaries in some cases. And, but, you better not have a system that is dependent on the absence of fraud. (laughs) It will be with us.

**INTERVIEWER:** What about, you know, another thing that we, I think we've seen in the last ten years was different was a lot of financial institutions before used to originate loans and, you know, how novel, carry them on their books. But now we see, you know, the proliferation of mortgage brokers, originate to distribute models, the street packages and securitizes, sends it off to someone else who maybe either keeps it or throws it into CDO and so on and so on. Any opinions on that relative change in the way that mortgage assets are originated?

**WARREN BUFFETT:** No, people will be more careful with their own money than with other people's money. And you can argue that Freddie and Fannie were the ones, you know, they started securitizing in effect and in a huge way people got used to buying mortgage instruments where they were very divorced from the origination of it. So there's no question that if there'd been a law against laying off mortgages to somebody else that you wouldn't have the same situation. You might not have as much, a lot of good things did happen in the country too, there was a-balancing the two, I'm not sure I could do but I can tell that more mischief will occur if somebody in Norway is buying a mortgage in Omaha than if some guy here is lending his own money. (laughs)

**INTERVIEWER:** There certainly appeared to be a loosening of underwriting standards and certainly an increase in what we've termed non-traditional mortgage product whether it's lower down payments, whether it's the liar loans, stated income loans, whether it's option arms, whether it's 228s, 327s, etc., etc. Any views on whether that had any?

**WARREN BUFFETT:** Oh, it had had plenty to do, I mean, it fuelled, it fuelled extreme leverage and it fuelled leverage that could only be paid out of the re-sale of the asset rather than the income of the borrower and once you start lending money big time to people where your hope of getting your money back is that the asset goes up rather than the asset produces enough to service the loan, I mean, that very nature whether it's farmland, whether it's oil in Texas, you know, it creates a lot of problems.

**INTERVIEWER:** Any views on why we saw the growth in that kind of non-traditional mortgage product?

**WARREN BUFFETT:** We believed that, you know, houses were going to go up. Once you think the asset will go up you don't look to anything to anything else. And it became, because it had been going up, an awful lot of people believed it had to keep going up. I mean, it gets back to the nature of bubbles.

**INTERVIEWER:** We, I mean, from people we've talked to and articles we've read, I mean, we've heard people talk about or read that, you know, there was a lot of money coming into the U.S. chasing yield. There was the Street wanting it because of the change from buy and hold to the securitization model. Were Fannie and Freddie, you know, changing their purchasing patterns and increasing demand for non-traditional mortgage product for whatever reasons. Any comments on any of those possibilities?

**WARREN BUFFETT:** The market system creates incentives to do more business. (laughs) That is the nature of it. And, but I, you know, and people talk about excess funds around the world and all that. I tend to discount that sort of thing. But I don't discount the incentives that everybody in the American public from wanting to do a piece of business if they can do it tomorrow. Doesn't mean that they're terrible people or anything but what, you know, if I'm a realtor and I've seen a house go from $250 to $500,000 do I say to the person, now, this buying the house at $500,000 is kind of dumb because--it just doesn't happen. They say, you know, you better do it today because it's going to be more tomorrow. And so everybody gets into the act, doesn't mean they're evil people. There are some crooks in the process, but overall what happened was not caused by the crooks. It may have caused the crooks to get rich (laughs), a lot of it but it in my view was caused by a mass delusion.

**INTERVIEWER:** Throughout the '90s and the 2000s members of Congress, members of the administration were all encouraging home ownership.

**WARREN BUFFETT:** Sure.

**INTERVIEWER:** Both through statements, through plans and policies. How much of that do you think contributed to the bubble?

**WARREN BUFFETT:** It all contributes, but the truth is I've told people, home is a good investment, you know. Particularly if, it's got values beyond what it will do in terms of possible appreciation over time. It really is a way to go short on the dollar. I mean, if you borrow a fair amount of money it gets and most people don't have a good way of being short on the dollar and it's a pretty sound policy to be short dollars as long as you're carrying costs aren't too high. And when interest rates get low the carrying costs are not high. So it is not an unintelligent thing to do. It's only, it's only when it gets into this bubble aspect that it becomes unintelligent. But I would recommend today, you know, if a couple can afford it and you're not paying silly prices in terms of replacement value or things like that and you want to buy a home in Omaha, I would say, you know, have you found the neighborhood you wanted and you're going to, your family's going to live there and right now I think mortgage rates are very attractive, I would say buy it. But I wouldn't say buy three more on speculation and I wouldn't say buy it if it's going to take 50% of your income to service the mortgage. It's a sound idea that went crazy.

**INTERVIEWER:** Should it be a government policy to encourage home ownership?

**WARREN BUFFETT:** Well, I don't think, I would say it should be a government policy and we've got it through and Fannie and Freddie, we say we're in the mortgage business as a country. To help people who are following sound practice in the one way, I do not see anything wrong with having a government guarantee program that kicks in when people really have a 20% down payment, really only putting only 30% or so of their income into it. Still people are going to lose their homes for unemployment reasons and death and divorce and disability. I mean, the three Ds. But that's not going to cause a systemic problem. And more people are going to benefit from that program by far than anybody's going to be hurt by it. So I think that the government has a place in that and around the world has a place in it. But I don't think that if you're going to get 20% down payments that you should then take deals on the 3% down payments and then lay off that on some mortgage insurer or something like that. You don't want to encourage people to do things that are going to cause them pain later on. And you're going to have occasional pain for unemployment but, you know what, you don't want system-wide pain because you've encouraged them to do things that are stupid.

**INTERVIEWER:** One of the areas in our statute is the role of monetary policy and of course a lot of folks have commented on the low level of interest rates throughout the 2000s. Any view on that as a contributing cause?

**WARREN BUFFETT:** Well, it makes it obvious, it makes it easier but no, I don't think that was what caused this. You couldn't have had it if you'd had 15% rates obviously. But it all, you know, it all worked together, you know. And finally the fact that houses kept going up a lot. It just, you know, put a model in people's minds. You have 300 million Americans have got a economic model in their mind and you say, Moody's is dumb for having it and S&P is dumb for having it but it was pervasive.

**INTERVIEWER:** Another area in the statute that we're directed to look at and we have been looking at of course is the role of accounting and specifically mark-tomarket rules on accounting. I know you wrote in your shareholder letter or letters that, you know, the mark-tomarket accounting rules result in wild swings in your derivative accounting but that you and Mr. Munger and what it is-

**WARREN BUFFETT:** We explain it, it is our job to explain it.

**INTERVIEWER:** Right, but do, and other people we've talked to and articles we've read have talked about, you know, the mark-tomarket accounting rules if nothing else perhaps fueling the downward spiral, you know, in the '07 and '08 timeframe when folks got into liquidity crunches and had to sell assets, etc. Any views on the role of accounting and mark-tomarket accounting?

**WARREN BUFFETT:** I'm less religious about it than I used to be (laughs). I, because, well, you know, after '29 in the insurance business they put in so-called, I forget, they had a term for it but I think it was called, basically it commissioned evaluations of some sort. And they did not make insurance companies write their stuff down because they said, you know, you're basically putting them all out of business and these are temporary things. And the truth was it probably benefited the country that they didn't liquidate all the insurance companies in the early '30s based on what would have, in effect, been mark-to-market accounting. I still, there's so much mischief when you get away from mark-to-market that I, that I'm still a believer in it but I can see where, I can see certain situations where it might have sort of anti-social effects as well. Getting back to derivatives, I mean, what has always struck me as extraordinary is that you basically have four big auditing firms in the country. And I would guarantee you that they are attesting to the statements affirmed where they have both sides of a derivative transaction and there is a different value being put on them by the two parties. And they're signing them, I mean, we're talking big numbers sometimes, too. It'd be interesting to take the million contracts or whatever they, a couple of million J.P. Morgan, and find two firms that have the same auditor and compare the valuations. (laughs)

**INTERVIEWER:** It might have been a good survey for us. You know, I mean, an area we somewhat touched on that's really, leverage and liquidity are just capital requirements for financial institutions. Were they too low, are they too low?

**WARREN BUFFETT:** It's very tough, it's very tough because there's such a difference in how when institutions can be doing, you know, I mean, just take the derivatives book, I mean. How do you measure that compared to straight loans? I mean, are you going to only take the netted off, non-collateralized balance finally, I mean, the residual and say that's the only exposure you have or are you going to weight some for netting, you know, but only compounds it at 10%. It is very tough and, we're going to have higher capital standards in all likelihood but knowing what to measure against and all that, it's just a very difficult problem. And, of course, partly that was solved by people using ratings. And, you know, and the extraordinary thing, if you look at the AIG and my memory is and again, I'm doing all this from memory, my memory is that they got up to like a number of 300 billion of what they call regulatory arbitrage where it enabled largely German banks or certainly European banks to carry less capital against their loans since AIG was guaranteeing those loans against loss and AIG had a triple A rating therefore that carried over into lower capital requirements abroad. And they were getting paid practically nothing for them and they thought they were running no risk at all. But it was a ratings arbitrage, basically, it was, they called it regulatory arbitrage. But it was based on what ratings required in the way of capital requirements. But, you know, the regulators got a terrible job too, I mean, how do you deal with all these people doing different things and come up with some kind of standard that says what they have to maintain in the way of capital. I don't envy them the job.

**INTERVIEWER:** You, an argument you often hear on the other side from institutions that don't want higher capital requirements is it's going to impact us competitively across the globe. Any views on that response?

**WARREN BUFFETT:** It would, it would. I mean, just take it to the extreme. If you said that every in the bank in the United States had to have 30% capital and every bank in Europe has 3% capital, you know. To earn the same returns on capital (laughs), they can work on much narrower margins than the American bank. That doesn't mean you don't do it but leverage is a competitive tool in terms of achieving returns on equity. That's why it has to be guarded against.

**INTERVIEWER:** Any views on what the right capital levels are for financial institutions?

**WARREN BUFFETT:** It's more complicated than that.

**INTERVIEWER:** Believe me, I know.

**WARREN BUFFETT:** Okay. (laughter)

**INTERVIEWER:** Is imposing some kind of leverage restriction and [unintelligible] the risk something that, looking back before banks were able to get into more exotic businesses, you know, 30, 40, 50 years ago, is that something that you think should be a function of government through regulation or is that if Greenspan two years ago, is that something that the market could police itself in some way?

**WARREN BUFFETT:** I don't believe the market polices itself, I mean, Greenspan is a friend of mine but he's read more of Ayn Rand than I have, I mean, I'll put it that way. (laughs) So I do not believe the markets police themselves in matters of leverage and other matters. I do, that's why I get back to the incentives of the person. I mean, that makes a difference. It doesn't solve everything, I mean, you can still get terribly optimistic managements that will do very stupid things and all that. But if I had a choice between setting the capital standards and setting the management incentives and that were my only choice with banks, I would rather set the management incentives.

**INTERVIEWER:** One of the things we've seen and that I've seen from my previous life as a bank examiner, we particularly saw with the broker dealers was the liquidity issue of their asset liability mismatch. And particularly, you know, that they were, had a lot of short term money.

**WARREN BUFFETT:** It's the nature of the national institutions both life insurance companies and banks. The, no capital requirements protect you against a real run. I mean, if your liabilities all are payable virtually that day or I should say virtually all your liabilities are payable that day, you can't run a financial institution and be prepared for that. And that's why we've got the Fed and the FDIC. I mean, you can't stand, if you're a life company or a bank, you can't stand around, you can be the most soundly capitalized firm in town but if I hire, if there were no FDIC and the Fed and you had a bank capitalized with 10% of capital and I had one with 5% of capital and I hired 50 people to go over and start standing right in front of your bank, you're the guy that's going to fail first. Then when get through with you they're going to come over to my bank too, that's why we don't do that sort of thing because you can't contain the fire over on the other guy's bank. But you can't, you can't stand a run. So you need the Federal Reserve and the FDIC. And even with Northern Rock, the UK government and came and said we guarantee everything they still had lines. I mean, when people are scared they're scared. And there is no reason to leave, I mean, if you see if it's uninsured and you see a line at a bank where you've got your money, get in line. (laughs). You know, buy a place from the guy that's first in line if necessary, you know. And even if you're at another bank, get in line there and take your mad money and put it under a mattress. You can always put it back a week later as long as there no penalties, why in the world, you know. That's why we got a Fed and an FDIC and I think it's one of the, you know, I think the FDIC and Social Security were the two most important things that came out of the '30s. I mean, the system needed an FDIC.

**INTERVIEWER:** What did you do, you know, this is, you're raising the issue really of the shadow banking system, the parallels unregulated without FDIC insurance or any other form of insurance other than until they stepped in and guaranteed money market funds as the short term stability and confidence raiser. What did Berkshire Hathaway do with all of its cash, I mean, you don't have --.

**WARREN BUFFETT:** That's a very good question because we were, for example, in

September in 2008 we faced, I think it was October 6th or something like that we had to come up with six and a half billion for our Wrigley deal. I was only going to have that in treasury bills even if I had got a minus yield because I had to come up with it. And I didn't know for sure, whether on October 6th, you know, what the situation would be with any bank. Now I thought it was 99.99% that it'd be fine, but I didn't think it was 100%. And I may bring along to the hearing, I sold a treasury bill in December 2008 for $5,000,090 and it was a $5,000,000 treasury bill due in April-something where the guy was going to get $5 million. So he was saying that the treasury bill was $90 better than his mattress. I mean, he could have put the $5 million under his mattress and then 90 bucks better off in April than he was by buying the treasury bill. Well, that's the way I felt too. I don't, I still feel that way incidentally. I mean, we don't have a whole list of approved short term investments around here. We have got treasury bills basically and treasury has the right, and is going to print money if necessary and that is triple A, I'm willing to go on the record on that. (laughs).

**INTERVIEWER:** That'll give you a rating yourself. (laughter)

**WARREN BUFFETT:** But nobody else is triple A in my mind, you know. And if we're really going to protect ourselves if we're not going to, we need to have real money. And now, I let the smaller operations just for matters of convenience do other things. But in terms of the vast chunk of what we have around here it's treasury and it will stay that way. Because I don't know what can happen tomorrow. I don't know if there's a, you know, pick any kind of a hugely disruptive--that's what you have to worry about are the discontinuities and there will be one someday. They closed the stock exchange in 1914, you know, for many months. They closed it for a few days after 9/11 but who knows what happens tomorrow.

**INTERVIEWER:** Speaking of that uncertainty, do you think in the financial crisis the government created some uncertainty by for instance stepping in and orchestrating the deal between J.P. Morgan and Bear whereas not stepping in or at least not stepping in sufficiently to orchestrate a deal for Lehman. Do you think that created uncertainty in the market for market participants?

**WARREN BUFFETT:** Yeah, there's no question that you would have expected, having seen them step in at Bear you would have expected to see them step in at Lehman. So when they didn't step in at Lehman, the world panicked. Now it had all these repercussions too in that Lehman commercial paper was held by money market funds and 30 million Americans held money market funds and if you get 30 million Americans worried about whether their money market funds are going to be worth 100 cents on the dollar, they're not going to buy anything, I mean. So they, you know, you create a tsunami, but, and most interestingly, of course, is if Ken Lewis hadn't have bought Merrill on Sunday, I think the system would have stopped, you know. He is (laughs) the guy that turned out to have saved the system. He paid a crazy price in my view, well he could have bought it the next day for nothing because Merrill was going to go when Lehman went. So the government was going to have to step in some place and you can argue that they probably should have stepped at Lehman but I would say this, I consider overall the behavior of Paulson and Bernanke and Sheila Bair and even though I'm not a Republican, even the President, I consider them to have done a terrific job during that period. I mean, you don't call everything right and if they made a mistake on Lehman they corrected it. And they did everything they could to correct it very quickly and if they hadn't have done that and if Ken Lewis the B of A, we would have, the system would have stopped. It stopped a little bit for a short period anyway. But what we saw fall off into the economy subsequently was nothing compared to I think what would have happened otherwise.

**INTERVIEWER:** And following up on that the commercial paper market. You've alluded to what happened in the commercial paper market there. Any thoughts in terms of additional safeguards or anything that could remedy what had happened in-

**WARREN BUFFETT:** Pretty tough. We don't buy commercial paper. But I do believe if you ran into a similar situation today the government would guarantee commercial paper, they'd have to. And that's the important part. You have to believe the federal government will act and they will act promptly, decisively and all that sort of thing. That became, I guess, a little bit of a, more than a little bit of a question, significant question after Lehman. The treasury and the Fed remedied that very quickly by taking, in my view, by taking action. I said it was economic Pearl Harbor, but we sent out, you know, we sent out the fleet the next day, but we had the ships in the harbor unfortunately when the day Lehman failed. (laughs) But you saw one of the first TARP type arrangement got defeated in Congress what happened in the market. I mean, Congress was the big fear with, I think, was the biggest fear with the American public at that time.

**INTERVIEWER:** How do you draw the line for determining where the government should intervene for specific institutions and not.

**WARREN BUFFETT:** Well, I think they did it right in Bear, I mean they wiped out the stockholders pretty much, I mean, you lost 180 down to 10 as it turned out. But if Paulson had his way it would have been $2 or less. You wiped out the shareholders. Now again, you know, the management, Jimmy Cayne lost a lot of money, but he's a rich man. And so that did not set a good lesson for the rest of the world in my idea but you send a big lesson in terms of the shareholders. And I think if the government has to decide, if troubles are brewing the government should err on the side of overkill.

**INTERVIEWER:** How would you decide though between stepping in on Bear and not stepping in on ACME or another financial institution. How do you draw the line in your mind?

**WARREN BUFFETT:** Well, with banks it's easy because the FDIC can handle everything except Citigroup and BofA, I mean. They handled Wachovia in their own way, they handled WaMu. I mean, we had 8% or 9% of the deposits of the United States change hands without the federal government getting involved even. But the FDIC could not have, they participated in the situation with Citi, but Citi would have been probably too much. Wachovia was the third largest in the country and they got it done. So, stepping in, you don't need to worry about stepping in on institutions around here, but the chance to step in on Freddie and Fannie there wasn't any question about that. And then you get-- they really didn't need to step in, if they did with Morgan Stanley or Goldman Sachs or Wells Fargo. But they did need to get the system, they needed to give the American public the confidence that they would do whatever it took. Now those firms didn't need it as long as the system didn't totally collapse. But as part of convincing the world that the system wasn't going to totally collapse that they were part of the movie that took place.

**INTERVIEWER:** We're very close to being done because we started a little bit early so I thank you. A couple of questions. Do you

have any sense as to what the difference between what's going on in Europe is and what
went on in Europe is and what happened here
because clearly Europe didn't have the same
kind of crisis happening.

**WARREN BUFFETT:** It's true. It's very different, it's an even more interesting movie
(laughs) and since this is on tape somebody
will find how it all plays out. I don't know how
it'll play out. It's a different situation in that
in the United States we were saving ourselves.
And we wanted to be saved and we wanted
Washington, we knew only the government
could save us basically at the time from a
colossal collapse. And even with that a year
and a half later a lot of people are mad at the
people who participated in doing it when all
we were doing was trying to save ourselves we
weren't trying to save Mexico. It wasn't like
we had a North American union where we all
were tied to the same currency and Mexico's
problems were--can you imagine what the re-
action if we'd, if we'd been saving Mexico in-
stead of the United States to the legislature or
the regulators who were involved. So Europe,
they have to act big but they have a, they have
a system where a group of people are going
to have to be helping another group. Now we
all think we're Americans so when America is

saving America we, that can be pretty cohesive. But although like I say, it's still recriminations, all kinds of things have come out of it. Now you picture Europe where you've got a group of people that are being asked perhaps to put up a lot of money and perhaps bear a lot of burdens perhaps incur inflation to help another group who they don't think have been behaving the way that they would have behaved. And they don't really have the, you know, ethnic social connection, I think it's really problematic what happens.

**INTERVIEWER:** But do you think there are any parallels in how their problem developed or is it really a European problem as opposed to a housing bubble?

**WARREN BUFFETT:** Probably [unintelligible] because in the end, for a long time everybody thought they were all equal and if you got a Euro denominated bond it didn't make difference or a deposit from any one of 16 countries it was the same then and all of sudden the market perceiving that it wasn't the case. And once people started thinking about it, they realized it really wasn't the case. And this thing's only been around for, you know, less than 15 years or whatever it is. And they start thinking maybe I better line up at that bank. And they don't have to do it physically they start pushing little buttons and the money starts moving around and all of a sudden 16 countries have a problem where they think, most of them think they weren't part of it. And that is, could be enormously contagious. No one has to buy a Greek bond, nobody has to buy a Spanish bond. Now usually when, in America, the central bank has to buy, it'd be a roundabout process but (laughs) we know somebody will buy U.S. bonds tomorrow because we've got a central bank that's totally in sync with the interests of the country. And we'll print money if necessary. And nobody, Greece doesn't have the power to print, you know, they'd be fine if their obligation [unintelligible] It's a very, very interesting problem and I won't predict how it will come out because you've got a tape (laughs) and I'd look very dumb later on.

**INTERVIEWER:** So you have any books that you'd like that have been written on the crisis? I know that Sorkin has worked with-

**WARREN BUFFETT:** Sorkin has written a very good book. I mean, there have been a number of good books. The book I would write if I was in the writing business, I would write a fictional book and my book would probably be titled something like, If Ken Lewis Hadn't Answered the Phone, and then

I would go from there forward with Merrill falling on Monday and describing what the world would have looked like. It'd be a hell of a book. (laughs) I'm not sure what the ending would be but, you know, he got that call on Saturday, he gets a fairness opinion in 24 hours from two guys who are getting $10 million each. Is the fairness buy Merrill Lynch at $29 a share which, I mean-

**INTERVIEWER:** Chris Flowers.

**WARREN BUFFETT:** Chris Flowers and another firm that is affiliated with Chris Flowers. And do you think Chris Flowers would have paid $29 or $2.90 for Merrill Lynch on Sunday? (laughs) You know, it's an interesting world, but it may have saved the system some terrible acts. May have actually saved the system.

**INTERVIEWER:** Okay. Well.

**WARREN BUFFETT:** I don't expect, if you decide to write that book, I don't expect any royalties. (laughs)

**INTERVIEWER:** At the rate we're going it'll take a long time. Well, thank you.

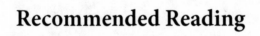

# Recommended Reading

# Recommended Reading

How I made $2,000,000 in the Stock Market
   *By: Nicolas Darvas*

Wall Street: The Other Las Vegas
   *By: Nicolas Darvas*

You Can Still Make it in the Market
   *By: Nicolas Darvas*

How I Made Money Using the Nicolas Darvas System,
Which Made Him $2,000,000 in the Stock Market
   *By Steve Burns*

The Battle for Investment Survival
   *by Gerald M. Loeb*

The Psychology Of The Stock Market
   *by G. C. Selden*

The Science of Getting Rich
   *by Wallace D. Wattles*

Think and Grow Rich
   *by Napoleon Hill*

*Available at www.bnpublishing.net*

CPSIA information can be obtained at www.ICGtesting.com
Printed in the USA
LVOW081625170712

290453LV00001B/109/P